Hangover Remedies
of a Broken Heart

David Orta

BookLeaf Publishing

India | USA | UK

Presentation by *BookLeaf Publishing*

Web: www.bookleafpub.com

E-mail: info@bookleafpub.com

ISBN: 9789360943776

First edition 2024

*To the family members that were lost
throughout the journey.*

A String You Can Not See

There was an invisible string between us miles
apart.
This theory understood by some and known by
little,
until you are the few that see it shortened.
As we have conversations,
we figured out all the places that almost aligned
for us:

Coffee shops,
Renaissance fairs,
Warped tours,
Amusement parks,

The list
goes on
and
on...

We begin to laugh at the differences in time,
or how one of us went right instead of left.
Hidden in plain sight,
but circumstances stopped us from seeing each
other.
As if the world waited for the day we met;
when you saw me and told me everything.

My Next Career Path

If my past relationships were on a resume,
I would be accused of job hopping.
Not because I can't hold a job;
the policies just change and I get replaced.

Which is a drag.
I loved my last job.

I wanted to get promoted, CEO with a corner
office.
But, someone else took the position and
now I want a career change.

Should I go back to applying or
commit to an early retirement?

Go to the Love and Lost department:
turn in my pink slip (just a bullet)
and finally do my last exit interview.
While it travels across my brain,

The person who loved and truly lost.
I can finally be happy with my last position.

Texting on Valentine's Day

The worst part about love
is that it could end.
With a simple phone call,
or a text they send.
And it says,
"You could still be my best friend"
Of course you want to cry,
but the voice in your head says "pretend..."
So you do,
and you begin
to bend.
Because you wanted to spend the rest of your
life as a lover,
not a friend.
But some loves are not made to comprehend.
So you just reply and say,
"Happy Valentine's Day!"

How Did She Get In?

Sitting in my seat
Waiting for an idea to call
Suddenly, I see a woman with three faces
standing by my feet
She was about six feet tall and she made me feel
small

I could not think of a thing to say
But I started to think
How did she get in, my doors have been locked
all day
And before I could blink

She bashed my brains in with her bare fist
Now I no longer exist

In a Nice Urn

If I were to simply decompose,
Would you miss me
Or would you just stand there with the rotten
smell touching your nose
Because you finally realize that you are free.

No more worries other than a burial fee
Just wondering if it is even worth putting me six
feet deep
But hopefully you would cremate me as easy as
counting to three
After that you can easily go to sleep.

Because the man you used to love
Is now on the shelf above.

The Girl In White

There is an old tale
From a man in jail
About how his bunkmate fell ill
From staring at a mirror while standing still.

He was hypnotized by a girl in white
Whose mouth emitted a hazy red light
She was speaking to him in Morse code
But before his mate could tell him, he explodes

The man who told this tale was sentenced to
death
And that night was hung until he drew his last
breath
Nobody believed his tale, but the cell is still
empty to this day
And the guards always seem to keep their heads
away.

Because even if the woman in white is not real
They do not want to blow up to chunks and be
the rats' next meal.

Rotting on Trash Day

I was always impressed by the way she killed
bugs
Simply swat a fly or stomp a cockroach
Without even batting an eye
Then I realized that one day
I will be the bug she casually murders
Another emotionless kill
That will be thrown in the garbage without a
care
And simply crushed and left to rot for an eternity
Or likely till trash day.

Modern Day Messaging

Messages I sent
Waiting for your input
Then getting a notification
That you took a screenshot of my text

Me getting all excited
Waiting for the critic of a lifetime
Unfortunately, you just pretend to care
Did not even take a glance of what I sent

Slowly realizing that I was just another message

You decided to leave on read

I Still Wish the Same Wish

The other day I found a coin on the ground
It was by a wishing well
Without any hesitation I picked it up
And flipped it in and before it fell in
I wished for your happiness
Because even if we are not together
Doesn't mean you do not deserve better

Shine Bright

You are the star
In this well-lit city
Where I stop looking up
So, I can look down
At you

Dreams Vs Reality

I dream of you while I'm awake
The idea of us still together
Sitting next to each other
At your favorite burger place
Sneaking kisses while at work when no one can
see
Falling asleep in each other arms while the cats
jump on us

Dreams do not meet reality

I'm awake while I still dream of you
The reality is that we are further apart
Sitting across from each other carefully,
So we do not touch
Sneaking weighted looks while at work so we
are professional
Falling asleep in my own bed that feels
unfamiliar
As I wait hours for a text that I do not deserve
anymore

Reality allows for us to daydream

Biased Mathematics

I deserve the type of love I had.
How I was becoming the man someone could
fall in love with.
Where I was no longer a problem,
but a part of an equation that kept growing.
It was multiplying into something no
mathematician would dare solve.

I miss the type of love I had.
Now that it is over,
I am constantly yearning.
Wanting to add myself to the equation of love
again.
But when you multiply anything by zero,
it will always become nothing.
It is over and I am regressing
Back to what I always knew I would become.
A negative integer.

3:18 pm on July 5th

Regardless
that you radiate heat
that even the sun would be jealous of
Whether I am lying next to you
by day
or by night
I will always be in love

The Love of Others are What
I Need Most

Though times get tough and I feel alone
I'm happy for the ones that are here the most
Even though I'm terrified of the unknown
It's better than becoming a ghost

Their advice may be gut-wrenching
It may leave my jaw clenching

However I must put my head high
Change my mind and do what's right
Even if my smile is a lie
And I drown myself with booze at night

Though times get tough and I feel alone
I'm happy for the ones that are here the most

Rat-like Tendencies

15

I used to give you kisses,
and now my lips touch the rim of a shot glass
filled with cheap whiskey.
I miss smoking cigarettes,
because I used to be able to call myself a rat.
I would say,
"This poison will kill me slower than any rat
trap ever could!"

Cup of Coffee

I now look forward to the taste of a freshly
brewed coffee
Touching my lips every waking moment
Because you decided to leave
And give someone else a taste of you

Will I be Remembered?

17

When people pass away
You remember them randomly through
conversation or old photos
Even from songs or bad jokes
Possibly a chemical imbalance
Then I thought, when I die,
What will I be remembered for?
Arguments that I caused
Heartaches I caused
Or simply nothing at all.

Another Way of Playing Baseball

I would let you grab a metal baseball bat
Knock a homerun into my ribs
Until four of them break; call it a grand slam
I'd cough up the blood
And even if you do not take me to get fixed up
I won't get mad at you
Because I'll convince myself that I deserve it

Flower Petals

When I was much younger
I used to pull petals off flowers
Then I would joyfully recite
"She loves me…"
"… she loves me not."
Pauses in between to imagine our make believe
Spending lavish hours on the start
Yet, I would always stop halfway
Because I never wanted to know the answer
Of how our make believe would end

A Belief

The Japanese believe that your present face is
the one you loved before.

I don't know who I used to love,
But I know who I love now.
And I hope to look as beautiful,
As you.

Self-titled

Hangover remedies of a broken heart
Is a short tale of the past ten years
Where I have loved
And lost
And loved
And lost all over again
Where I thought being "witty" or "smart" would
fix the problems that arose
Instead, it was a bandaid on a wound
That's why there is no rhyme or funny remark,
I am stating what I believe you should know
Now that this is the end and you have more
questions than answers
However, you will get none.